GREAT STORYTELLERS
PAM MUÑOZ RYAN
Erinn Banting
AV2
www.openlightbox.com

Step 1
Go to **www.openlightbox.com**

Step 2
Enter this unique code
SHIFYL1Y4

Step 3
Explore your interactive eBook!

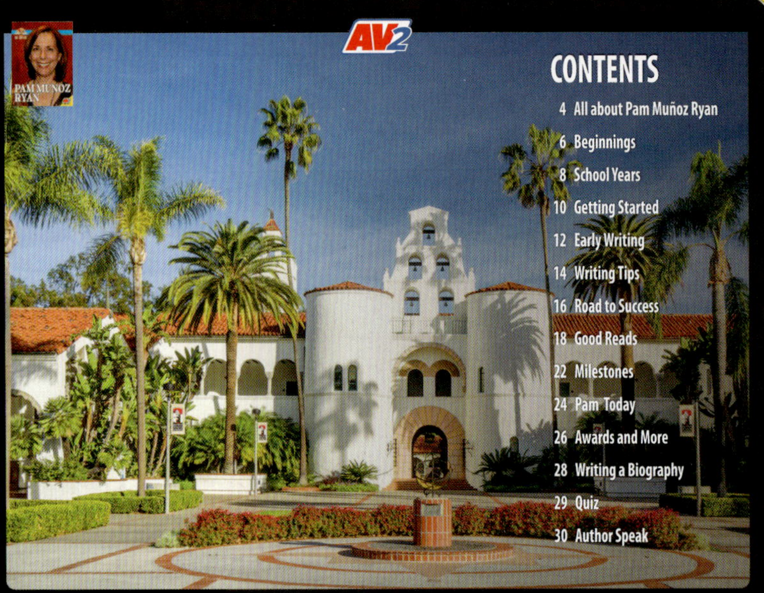

AV2 is optimized for use on any device

Your interactive eBook comes with...

Contents
Browse a live contents page to easily navigate through resources

Audio
Listen to sections of the book read aloud

Videos
Watch informative video clips

Weblinks
Gain additional information for research

Slideshows
View images and captions

Try This!
Complete activities and hands-on experiments

Key Words
Study vocabulary, and complete a matching word activity

Quizzes
Test your knowledge

Share
Share titles within your Learning Management System (LMS) or Library Circulation System

Citation
Create bibliographical references following APA, CMOS, and MLA styles

This title is part of our AV2 digital subscription

1-Year K–5 Subscription
ISBN 978-1-7911-3320-7

Access hundreds of AV2 titles with our digital subscription.
Sign up for a FREE trial at **www.openlightbox.com/trial**

Contents

All about Pam Muñoz Ryan

Pam Muñoz Ryan has written books for both adults and children. Her stories are read and loved around the world. Pam writes about strong characters who face challenges. In the process, they learn about themselves.

Many of the heroes in Pam's books are female. She writes about people who changed history or who changed her life. Other characters she writes about are fictional. They have come from Pam's own imagination.

Pam mostly writes for readers ranging in age from 4 to 18. She has authored picture books as well as full-fledged novels.

Pam has written more than 40 books.
Pam's books have been translated into more than 12 languages.

Beginnings

Pam was born on December 25, 1951. She grew up in Bakersfield, California. Esperanza, or Hope, Bell was Pam's mother. She worked at a high school library. Pam's stepfather, Donald Bell, worked as a delivery truck driver. Pam thought of Don as her real dad.

Pam had two younger sisters. She also had 22 younger cousins on her mother's side. Her grandmother, Esperanza Muñoz, lived nearby. Esperanza was from Mexico. Grace Bell, Don's mother, lived in Arvin, California. She was from Oklahoma. Pam and her sisters were close to their big, lively family.

Pam visited one of her grandmothers every Saturday. Both grandmothers told Pam stories. Grace told stories from her life in Oklahoma and sang country songs. Esperanza told her stories in Spanish. She also took the family to weddings and picnics. At these events, Pam learned about her family's rich past. She was raised to be proud of her Mexican roots.

Where Pam Was Born

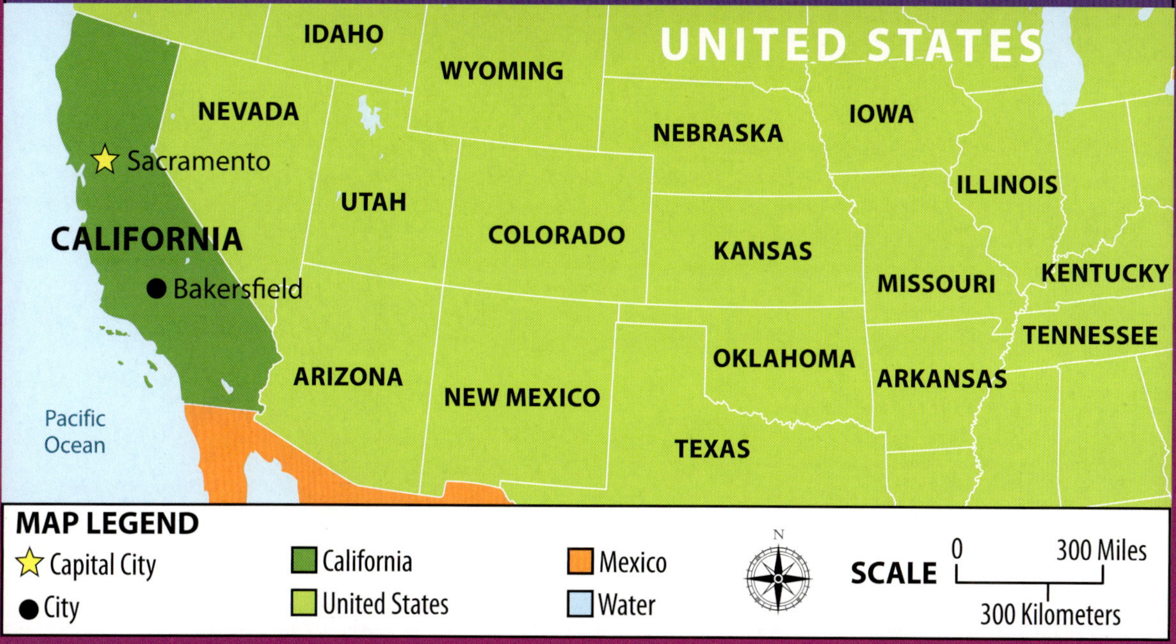

Bakersfield is found in the southern part of California, about two hours north of Los Angeles. It has a population of about 407,000 people.

School Years

Pam learned to read before she started school. Her grandmother, Esperanza, had a set of encyclopedias that Pam enjoyed reading. Each book in the set was filled with interesting facts.

As a child, Pam loved to use her imagination. She would make up stories, which her sisters and cousins would then act out. She also loved to play different games. In some, she would be a doctor. She also liked to pretend to be an explorer.

When Pam was in Grade 5, her family moved across town. She had to leave her friends behind. Pam had a hard time at her new school. She did not feel like she fit in. Many of her new classmates had been friends with each other since kindergarten.

Reading made Pam feel less lonely. She would hop on her bike and go to the local library as often as she could. Pam liked to imagine she was the characters in the books she found there. She could be Anne Shirley, the main character in *Anne of Green Gables*, or one of the characters from the Little House on the Prairie books.

The Little House on the Prairie books were written by Laura Ingalls Wilder and told the story of her family's life as pioneers in 19th-century America. The books were made into a television series that ran from 1974 to 1983.

Getting Started

After completing her elementary grades, Pam began attending Washington Junior High. The school had a newspaper. Pam's love of writing helped her get a job as the newspaper's **editor**. She played an important role in choosing the stories the paper covered. She was also assigned to write some of them.

In high school, Pam's strongest subjects were English and **composition**. Her love of reading, writing, and books gave her an idea. When she graduated from Grade 12, she wanted to be a teacher.

To become a teacher, Pam had to go to college. However, neither of her parents had gone to college. They did not understand why she wanted to go. The school Pam wanted to attend was also four hours away from home. This meant she would not be able to live at home while she studied. The cost of college **tuition** and living in another town was going to be very high. As concerned as Hope and Donald were, they supported their daughter and helped her with these costs. Pam also worked part-time to help pay for school.

All of her hard work paid off. In 1973, Pam graduated from San Diego State University (SDSU). She was ready to work with children and teach them to love books as much as she did.

San Diego State University was founded in 1897 as a teacher's college. Today, it provides studies in a range of subjects and has a student body of about 36,000.

Early Writing

After college, Pam found a job teaching children. She taught her students in both English and Spanish. One tool she used in her teaching was books. Pam loved reading to her students.

In 1975, Pam married Jim Ryan. A few years later, she and Jim started their family. They had two daughters and twin sons. While her children were young, Pam took a break from teaching to care for them.

Once her children were all school-aged, Pam went back to work. She taught at a daycare center during the day and took advanced teaching classes in the evenings. One of Pam's professors noticed Pam was an excellent writer. The professor asked Pam if she had ever thought about a career in writing.

Shortly after Pam graduated with her **master's degree** in education, a friend asked for her help with a book she was writing. The question from her professor came back to Pam. She had read thousands of books over the years. She knew how to tell a story. Pam decided it was time for her to try writing as a **profession**.

Pam was the first person in her family to graduate from college.

Pam wrote three books for adults before she began writing for children.

Pam taught preschool children who were in the Head Start program. This program provides education and other services to children from low-income families.

Writing Tips

When Pam writes, she thinks about the kinds of stories she likes to read. She uses this to guide her own writing. Her ideas often come from her own experiences and those of the people around her.

Start Reading

Pam believes that young writers should read as much as they can. Libraries are a great place to start. Pam reads for fun. She also reads to learn new things. Reading helps writers develop their own style. They can see how other people write. This helps them come up with ideas and a voice of their own.

Listen to People's Stories

Pam heard many wonderful stories from her grandmothers. She advises aspiring writers to listen to people's stories and write them down. Pam used some of her Grandmother Esperanza's stories in her book *Esperanza Rising*.

Write and Write Again

Writing a book is hard work. When Pam is working on a book, she writes every day. Pam sometimes says that she is not just a writer, but a rewriter as well. Pam rewrites her books as many as 30 times. Rewriting improves the story and the characters. It also helps writers practice. Practice will make their writing better.

Road to Success

Pam enjoyed writing stories for young children. However, it was very difficult for Pam to get her stories **published** at first. She would send them to publishers, only to have them rejected.

Then, Pam met Kendra Marcus. Kendra was a **literary agent**. She helped Pam sell her stories. Kendra also suggested that Pam add her family name, Muñoz, to her name to reflect her Mexican heritage.

With Kendra's help, Pam soon had her first published children's book. Released in 1994, it was called *One Hundred Is a Family*. The book teaches counting while also showing readers that there are many different kinds of families.

Next, Pam began to write books that taught children about history. The first was called *The Flag We Love*. It is about the history of the American flag and why the flag is important. Pam also wrote *California Here We Come!* Released in 1997, it included fun and interesting facts about Pam's home state.

In 2008, Pam's *California Here We Come!* book was re-released under a new title. This time, it was called *Our California*.

While researching information to put in *California Here We Come!*, Pam learned about a 19th-century woman named Charlotte Parkhurst. Charlotte had disguised herself as a man so that she could live the life she wanted. When Pam's editor, Tracy Mack, heard about Charlotte, she thought her story would make a good book. Tracy asked Pam if she had thought of writing longer books. Pam decided to try it. The story became *Riding Freedom*, Pam's first novel.

The Publishing Process

A **manuscript** goes through many stages before it is published. Often, authors change their work to follow an editor's suggestions. The final book can look very different from what the author first wrote.

Good Reads

Pam's stories have touched many people. She writes stories about people who overcome the problems they encounter. In doing so, Pam shows her readers that they can do the same.

Amelia and Eleanor Go for a Ride

Amelia Earhart was a famous **aviator**. Eleanor Roosevelt was a well-known **First Lady**. Both women were also close friends. One evening in 1933, Amelia and Eleanor decide to go flying. They did not let the fact that they were right in the middle of a White House dinner stop them. They did not even take the time to change out of their gowns. Adventure awaited, and they were ready to experience it.

Esperanza Rising

Esperanza Ortega has a very happy life in Mexico. Then, her family's fortune changes. It is the time of the **Great Depression**, and she and her mother must move to California. Esperanza faces many challenges in her new home. She needs to find work. She has to make friends in her new home. She has to keep her family together. Through all of this, Esperanza must also hold on to hope.

When Marian Sang

Singer Marian Anderson is known for her beautiful voice and for changing history. In 1939, she sang from the steps of the Lincoln Memorial, in Washington, DC. A crowd of approximately 75,000 people came to hear her sing. Her voice united people who were divided. This book tells the story of her life, struggles, and successes.

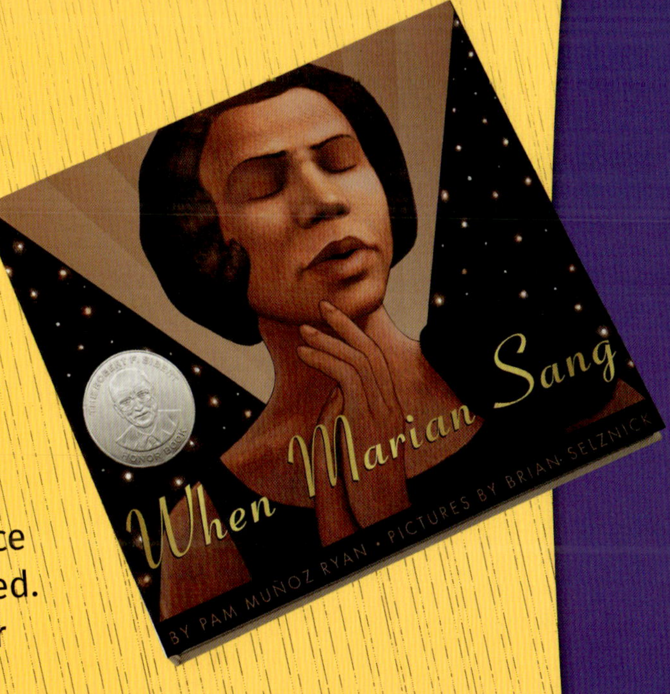

Paint the Wind

Maya does not have much left to help her remember her mother. She has a few memories, a photograph, and a box of toy horses. Now living with her grandmother, Maya has few freedoms. Far away in Wyoming, a wild paint horse named Artemisia must also escape. When she does, she faces a dangerous journey. Finally, she finds Maya. Together, they discover why Artemisia is so important to Maya and her past.

The Dreamer

The Dreamer tells the childhood story of Neftalí Reyes, who later became known as the famous poet, Pablo Neruda. Neftalí grew up in Temuco, Chile. From an early age, he knows that he has a very special gift. It is a gift that he cannot ignore, even when people mock him for it or when he begins to doubt it himself. To reach his destiny, he must stay true to the voice that he hears calling to him. This means learning more about the world around him and about himself.

Echo

Otto finds himself lost in a German forest. It is a place that is both mysterious and forbidden. There, he meets three sisters. The story is told from the point of view of four different characters. Each one is linked by history, a promise, and a magical harmonica.

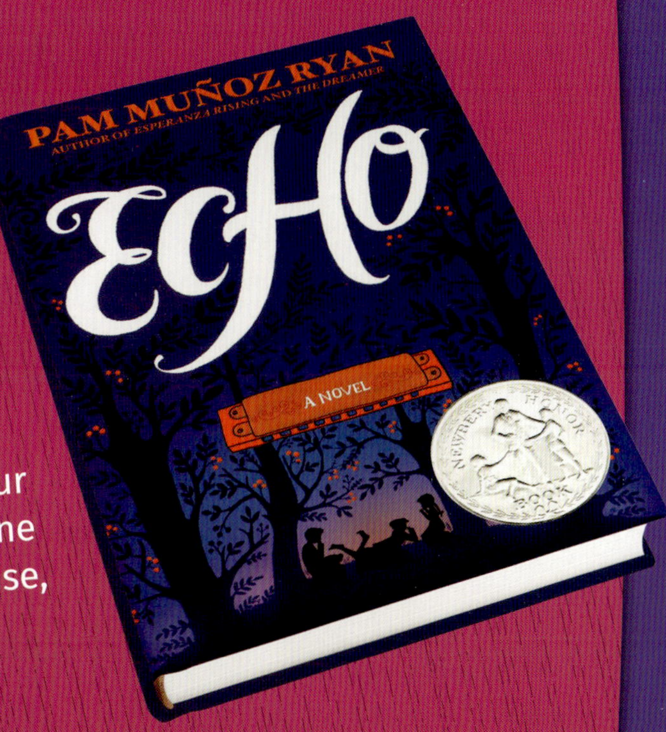

Mañanaland

Maximiliano, or Max, Córdoba loves **legends**. His favorite is the story of a gatekeeper. The gatekeeper has the power to guide people into the future, provided they are true of heart. When Max finds out a family secret, he decides to go on a journey of his own. If his heart is true, maybe he can discover what his future holds.

Milestones

Pam has put much effort into becoming a successful writer. Today, her books are read and taught around the world. Readers love her stories. They cannot wait to see what Pam comes up with next.

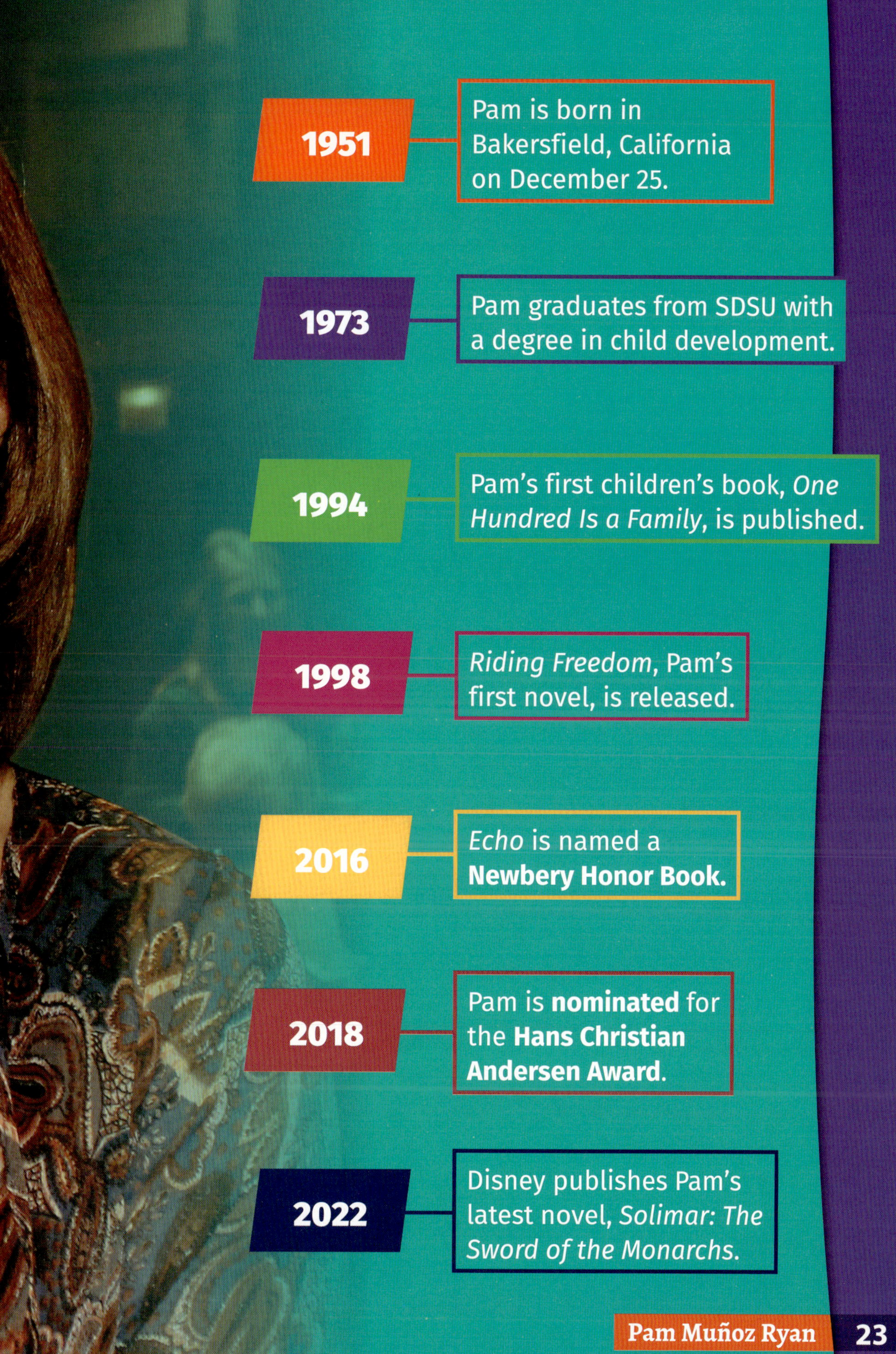

1951 — Pam is born in Bakersfield, California on December 25.

1973 — Pam graduates from SDSU with a degree in child development.

1994 — Pam's first children's book, *One Hundred Is a Family*, is published.

1998 — *Riding Freedom*, Pam's first novel, is released.

2016 — *Echo* is named a **Newbery Honor Book.**

2018 — Pam is **nominated** for the **Hans Christian Andersen Award**.

2022 — Disney publishes Pam's latest novel, *Solimar: The Sword of the Monarchs*.

Pam Today

Pam lives and works near San Diego. Her home is close to the Pacific Ocean. She likes to walk her dogs along the beach. Pam's children are now adults. Her children and five grandchildren visit her often.

Pam still teaches children about reading and books. She believes reading is very important and shares this message when she visits schools. Pam also gives **interviews** about her new books. She encourages children to learn and read as much as they can.

In 2022, Pam's new novel, *Solimar: The Sword of the Monarchs,* was released. It is about a Mexican princess who is on a mission to protect her kingdom's monarch butterflies. The book is the first in a series by Disney Publishing Worldwide. Pam's readers are excited to find out what happens to Solimar in the next book. They also hope Solimar will appear on the big screen someday.

The San Diego area has more than 70 miles of coastline. Its beaches attract people from around the world.

Awards and More

Pam and her books have won awards both in the United States and around the world. In 2016, Pam's novel *Echo* was named a Newbery Honor Book. This is one of the top prizes for children's books in the United States. Two years later, Pam was nominated for the Hans Christian Andersen Award, a major international award for children's literature.

Pam's readers have also celebrated her. When her novels come out, they are often on the *New York Times* list of best-selling books. Pam also won the International Literacy Association/Children's Book Council's Children's Choice award for *Echo*. Schoolchildren from across the United States choose the winners of this award from hundreds of books.

Pam's novel *Echo* also won the Booksource Scout Award, which recognized new books that had the potential to become children's classics.

Esperanza Rising was on *TIME* magazine's 2015 list of the 100 best books for young adults. It has sold more than 14 million copies. The book has even been made into a play. It has been performed at the Children's Theater Company in Minneapolis, the Goodman Theater in Chicago, and the Cutler Majestic Theater in Boston.

Minneapolis's Children's Theater Company is the largest children's theater in the United States and has won numerous awards for its programming. It is known for creating new works for young people.

Writing a Biography

All of the parts of a biography work together to tell the story of a person's life. Find out how these elements combine by writing a biography. Begin by choosing a person whose story fascinates you. You will have to research the person's life by using library books and reliable websites. If possible, you can also email the person or write him or her a letter. The person might agree to answer your questions directly.

Parts of a Biography

Early Life

- Where and when was the person born?
- What is known about the person's family and friends?
- Did the person grow up in unusual circumstances?

Growing Up

- Who had the most influence on the person?
- Did the person receive assistance from others?
- Did he or she have a positive attitude?

Developing Skills

- What was the person's education?
- What was the person's first job or work experience?
- What obstacles did the person overcome?

Early Achievements

- What was the person's most important early success?
- What processes has this person used in his or her work?
- Which of the person's traits were most helpful in his or her work?

Person Today

- Has the person received awards or recognition for accomplishments?
- What is the person's life's work?
- How have the person's accomplishments served others?

Quiz

1 Where and when was Pam born?

2 What were the names of Pam's two grandmothers?

3 Where did Pam go to college?

4 In what year did Pam publish her first children's book?

5 What is the name of Pam's first novel?

6 How many books for adults did Pam write before becoming a children's writer?

7 How many children does Pam have?

8 Which one of Pam's books was made into a play?

ANSWERS

1. Bakersfield, California, on December 25, 1951 **2.** Esperanza and Grace **3.** San Diego State University (SDSU) **4.** 1994 **5.** *Riding Freedom* **6.** Three **7.** Four, two daughters and twin sons **8.** *Esperanza Rising*

Author Speak

The field of writing has its own language. Understanding some of the more common writing terms will allow you to discuss your ideas about books.

action: the moving events of a story

antagonist: the person in a story who opposes the main character

autobiography: a history of a person's life, written by that person

biography: a written account of another person's life

character: a person in a story, poem, play, or other work

climax: the most exciting moment or turning point in a story

episode: a scene or short piece of action in a story

fiction: stories about characters and events that are not real

foreshadow: to hint at something that is going to happen later in a story

imagery: a written description of a thing or idea that brings an image to mind

narrator: the speaker of a story who relates its events

nonfiction: writing that deals with real people and events

novel: published writing of considerable length that portrays characters within a story

plot: the order of events in a work of fiction

protagonist: the leading character of a story

resolution: the end of a story, when the conflict is settled

scene: a single episode in a story

setting: the place and time in which a story occurs

theme: an idea that runs throughout a story

Key Words

aviator: the operator or pilot of an aircraft

composition: the study of reading and writing concepts and skills

editor: a person who revises material for publication

First Lady: the wife or female partner of the U.S. President

Great Depression: a period of economic decline that lasted from 1929 to 1939

Hans Christian Andersen Award: the highest international recognition given to an author and an illustrator of children's books

interviews: structured conversations that gather information

legends: stories that have come down from the past

literary agent: a person who helps writers get their works published

manuscript: a draft of a story before it is published

master's degree: a qualification given to someone who has taken advanced studies at university

Newbery Honor Book: an award from the American Library Association to the author of one of the year's best American children's books

nominated: entered as a candidate for an award or honor

profession: a paid occupation

published: issued and distributed the work of an author

tuition: the price of or payment for instruction

Index

Get the best of both worlds.

AV2 bridges the gap between print and digital.

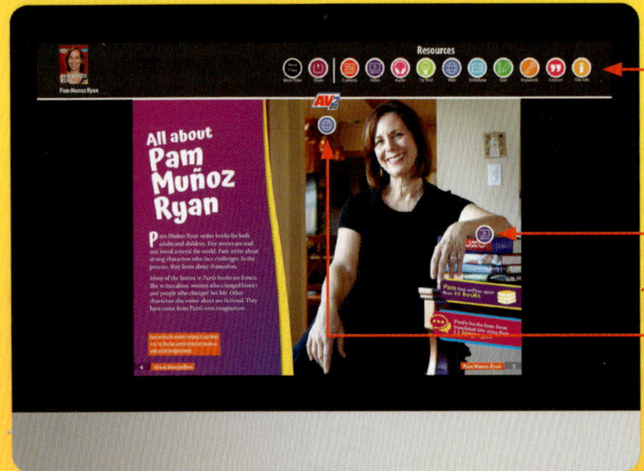

The expandable resources toolbar enables quick access to content including **videos**, **audio**, **activities**, **weblinks**, **slideshows**, **quizzes**, and **key words**.

Animated videos make static images come alive.

Resource icons on each page help readers to further **explore key concepts**.

Published by Lightbox Learning Inc.
276 5th Avenue
Suite 704 #917
New York, NY 10001
Website: www.openlightbox.com

Library of Congress Control Number: 2022947784

ISBN 978-1-7911-4839-3 (hardcover)
ISBN 978-1-7911-4840-9 (softcover)
ISBN 978-1-7911-4841-6 (multi-user eBook)

Printed in the Guangzhou, China
1 2 3 4 5 6 7 8 9 0 26 25 24 23 22

102022
101321

Project Coordinator: Heather Kissock Designer: Ana María Vidal

Every reasonable effort has been made to trace ownership and to obtain permission to reprint copyright material. The publishers would be pleased to have any errors or omissions brought to their attention so that they may be corrected in subsequent printings.

The publisher acknowledges Getty Images, Alamy, Newscom, Shutterstock, and Wikimedia as its primary image suppliers for this title.